The Secret Weapon
"A Dream Deferred"

Clyde E. Hall
Historian & Calculated Risk Taker

ISBN: 979-8-9874925-3-6

MTE Publishing
mtepublishing.com

Table of Contents

Chapters

Chapter 1

The Voice of Reason

My parents, Richard Sr. and Margaret Hall were married on April 14, 1948–a long time ago. Exactly five years after they were married, I made my debut, on April 14, 1953! I was the first boy and fourth child born within my parent's union. My half brother was born before my mom and dad met. My parents had two boys after my birth and all three of us were born three years apart. My sisters were born two years apart, then I came along and changed the arithmetic pattern.

My baby sister and I are "Irish Twins;" born 11 months apart. We are the same age for one month each year. When we both reached 46-years- old, she smugly smirked and said, "Well, how does it feel to be the same age as me for a whole month?" It felt the way it always felt… like she was my older sister.

Most young boys emulate their older brothers… I definitely emulated mine! He was my protector. However, he was also my harshest and most supportive critic at times.. I wanted to do mostly everything he did.

My brother and my oldest cousin frequently snuck off to the park across the street from our neighborhood. They were teenagers doing what teenagers did. However, me and my other boy cousin were only five- and six-years-old…

Naturally, they considered us "lil jits" and they didn't want us to "tag along."

Inevitably, my mom made my brother take me with him. My brother was quite perturbed. Reminiscing on the moment, I was a sight to see! I had on his pants, which swallowed me almost whole. My pant legs were rolled up multiple times and the waist was tucked in the same manner. I didn't have a belt. My hair wasn't brushed or combed, my face was dirty, and I was barefoot. To further complicate matters, their light complexion and curly hair allowed them to "pass" for something other than a little dirty pecan tanned Negro boy playing in a segregated Miami, Florida park in 1959.

There we were, living on SW 27th Street off Douglas Road in Miami. A street where every Black family was surrounded by white families. We were the grandchildren of Bahamian and Jamaican immigrants. The Bahamian Sweeting and Jamaican Hall families had united in holy matrimony and we now resided in the segregated south.

The Sweeting family was headed by patriarch, John V. Sweeting Sr. He purchased a large tract of land on SW 27th Street. He also owned land in Hallandale and Perrine, Florida. The intersection of SW 27th Street and Douglas Road was the location of their "Big House". My family's small development was known throughout Miami as Sweeting Town. The Sweeting family built their forever home while they lived in a small, shed-size room until the construction of the forever home was completed. My paternal grandfather married one of the Sweeting daughters and they also settled here.

Like their maternal grandfather, my dad and his brothers built our family a small wooden frame home. This home was located directly behind one of my dad's brother's homes. Initially our home had one bedroom for our parents and my three sisters, a living room, and a kitchen for seven people. Even though the home grew to two bedrooms, it never had a bathroom or a bedroom for my brothers and me. One day, I overheard my older siblings talking about moving away from home. We had been together ALL my life, where were they going?

This news agitated and hurt me! I had questions.

They're moving away, but why? Move to what? Move where? Why would I want to move away from Grandpa Hall? I could not imagine moving away from his banana pancakes and hot chocolate in the morning. I couldn't stand thinking of Grandpa's tall figure coming home and not having us run to greet him. When the other children went to school, I often observed Grandpa in admiration as he used his skills to repair household appliances or manicure the lawn. If I moved, I'd lose my bosom buddy, Gregory. He played make believe games with me like Superman, Batman, Cowboys and Indians, and the Lone Ranger. Who would ride old brooms and mop handle horses with me while shooting our six shooter cap guns?

The move meant big changes were on the horizon and I wasn't ready for that kind of change!

Who would I swing with so high I could kiss the sky? Jumping from the high-flying swings into the hot sands of the local park while happily screaming from the thrill of it. Would there be trees I could climb and race my cousins to the top to eat my fill of mangoes and other fruits? Who would help me make kites from newspapers, using old rags for the tail and palmetto branches for its frame? If we moved, Uncle John would not be able to give us a handful of nickels for us to buy ice cream from Mr.

Diamond, the Good Humor Ice Cream man.

There wouldn't be a constant flow of our relatives and friends regularly visiting each other! I already missed the laughing, eating, and playing until the darkness ran us home.

This move scared me to the point of experiencing nightmares. My anxiety was inescapable. I did not want to move—now or ever! I absolutely refuse!

Right on cue, my mom, the voice of reason, spoke as if she had read my mind and felt my deep consternation. My mom told me how a move meant that I would have "a bed to sleep in and a bathroom located directly across from my bedroom." She assured me that we wouldn't have one, but two bathrooms. I was further reminded that a new home would bring new challenges, new friends, a closeness to a different set of relatives, a new public school and a local shopping center that was walking distance from our new home.

My mom was that kind of person. She was able to see what troubled me without asking. She was able to calm my anxiety about the future because she highlighted the advantages in moving forward from Sweeting Town. My mom and dad didn't stop there because they did more than talk.

Chapter 2

Building Our Dream

I was comforted yet I still felt conflicted about the move. How could I be so sad, yet so happy all at the same time? Nevertheless, to ease our anxiety about the transition from our old home into our new home, our parents took us to our newly constructed house every Sunday as it was built from the ground up.

After church all nine of us piled into our 1955 Ford Fairlane. It was a four-door sedan. Dad drove us to Richmond Heights. It was a Miami suburb that was established primarily for the Black veterans and their families. The Black veterans had been denied the same GI benefits that were given to White veterans. Each home located in the area was in some stage of being built or was occupied within the last decade. Everyone who moved into our immediate vicinity would have to meet new people and learn and adjust to a relatively new community.

There were advantages and disadvantages of moving from the city to a suburb. This move meant we would no longer live in a wooden frame house, take baths in a #3 tin tub and/or shower at Grandpa's house. Moving meant that after six-and-a-half years, I would finally have my first bed, first bedroom and first bathroom. It also meant I wouldn't have to wait until everyone retired for the night, before my brother and I went to sleep on the sofa.

We would trade living close to Grandpa Hall for living near our maternal grandparents, Nathaniel and Ruth Gaiter. We also traded the short drive to our church for a longer ride across town on Sundays. Mom wouldn't have to catch multiple city buses to work at Kendall Hospital. Fortunately, she'd have the convenience of carpooling with some of our new neighbors. However, my dad's short commute to work would become much longer.

My brother traded a short car ride to high school, with dad, for a much longer car ride to school. My sisters and I traded a ride to elementary school for a walk to the neighborhood school. My older sister experienced the most stressful change of all when George Washington Carver Senior

High was changed from a senior high to a middle school. My two older sisters and others were then mandated by the Supreme Court to desegregate Palmetto and/or Killian Sr. High Schools. We had to make significant adjustments and adaptations so our new reality worked successfully.

"If there is no struggle, there is no progress..." ~ Frederick Douglas

My parents were middle and high school graduates. Even without college degrees they were wise enough to set the stage for the next act in our lives. They subtly crafted the proper mindset to prepare us to meet this new challenge of getting acclimated to this move.

In October of 1959, our family of nine moved out of our two bedroom, wooden frame house, with no restroom. Shortly thereafter, we settled into Richmond Heights. The community was founded by Air Force Captain Frank C. Martin to provide the opportunity for Black military and civilian families to have their slice of the American pie (homeownership). Our new house was a concrete block structure that consisted of three bedrooms and two baths with a living room and kitchen.

My maternal grandfather, Nathaniel C. Gaiter Sr., was a Navy veteran. He and his wife Ruth moved from Miami (Coconut Grove - Golden Gate) to the Richmond Heights community several years prior.

Granddaddy was serious, a no nonsense man, who sometimes stuttered when he was stressed or angry. He seemed to be able to grow fruit trees from a piece of cardboard and had the thickest and prettiest green grass I'd ever seen. His yard had fruit trees galore!

He would tear a motor apart and put it back together expecting it to start without hesitation. Out of the blue, he would hand me a Morgan Silver dollar from the 1800s or a Bulova wristwatch. I learned not to question him about things he gave me because he would simply take it back. And not only was he an armed forces veteran, but at one time, he was the only licensed Black plumber in Miami.

Grandma was the complete opposite. She was the definition of introvert—quiet, private, and reserved. She was a former teacher, so I couldn't drop the "th" from words and say dem, dose, dey or den without her immediate correction. She was patient with me and took her time modeling exactly what she expected me to say. Whenever I was disobedient, she immediately sent me home to my mama. She never raised her voice, lifted her hand to hit me, or spoke an angry word to me. My mom called Granny "one wise woman". She said Granny was one of the wisest persons she'd ever known. It was her eyes, not her voice that told you she was observing every move and detail. Like a computer, she would collect data and could tell you everything she saw; but she rarely did. I never saw a person master child psychology as effectively as she did!

Granny loved cane fishing on the banks of The Trail, Snapper Creek, and Dinner Key of Miami. She loved watching "Lawrence Welk", ballroom dancing and professional wrestling; she looked forward to watching them on Saturdays. Every Sunday, she attended Christ Episcopal Church and celebrated the Holy Eucharist. I think she loved her family more than all those things together. I cried like a baby when she died because she was, and still is, one of the lights of my world.

Even if cell phones, microwaves, computers, laptops, or other such technology existed when I was a child, we would not have had them because we could not afford them. We did not sit around eating snacks, watching TV, playing video games, or talking on the house phone because they didn't exist.

There was no air conditioning unit or heat pump in our home, so being inside wasn't comfortable. In fact, we only stopped playing outside if there was a rain or thunderstorm, or because nightfall was approaching. Before I knew it, Richmond Heights had grown on me. I embraced change and I was growing and glowing.

Change is the active ingredient that causes us to move from places of comfort. Change stretches and broadens our range of knowledge and understanding of who we are and those we share our lives with. Change in our lives helps form our environmental DNA.

I decided I will move. I will move. I will move! I'm enjoying the move!

North
1

Chapter 3

Smooth Move

After settling into the new area, I was shocked to learn we were living three doors down from my Uncle Lloyd and Aunt Barbara. This was great since we also lived less than a quarter mile from our maternal grandparents and several miles from our cousins in Perrine, another suburb. The heavens had opened and now I had six more boy cousins to play with within a five-mile radius and one of them was around my age.

Garrett, A.K.A. Pee Wee was almost a year older than me. We were about to get our play on. Pee Wee was all boy; a runt in size, but always trying to prove himself to others. He had a laser focus on those things that appealed most to him. Everything we did was competitive, but it was all in fun. I liked the fact that Garrett was older than me. He used his "seniority" to take his competitiveness to another level; thereby, improving my ability to stay on point during our shenanigans.

Our activities included building walking stilts of wood, playing marbles, foot racing, high jumping, climbing the tallest trees, looking for treasures in abandoned buildings, sliding down dirt hills on a piece of cardboard and eating as many two-for-a penny cookies and nickel candy we could buy.

Errrrr er er errrrrrrrrrrrr!!!!!!!

Once you decide to parachute from an airplane you can't stop falling to the earth. Our move was like parachuting from a plane and I had fallen in love with the new opportunities I anticipated.

I loved my new school, the neighborhood kids, how safe I felt everywhere in my community; this included feeling at ease in our home, school, neighborhood, church, and the local stores. There was no one there in 1959 trying to convince us that we were inferior or less than. There were no marches across Selma, no dogs ripping the flesh off little Black children, no policemen beating Black civil rights protesters with Billy clubs, no attempts to integrate our elementary school and no crosses burning on our front lawn.

The move afforded me the opportunity to connect with my cousins from the southern part of Miami more often. As a six-year-old boy, playing was something I liked to do as much as eating and sleeping. When I went to Perrine, no time was wasted finding something to do. If we could have gotten paid for playing, we'd be rich.

Introducing Jacket

Much talk had been made with my cousin Garrett about the jacket of many colors. Garrett and I were sworn to secrecy. After all, the Yellow Jacket was very special, for it had no owner. It was "wild" or considered free range in today's language. Imagine, a jacket which shined in the noon day sun like a room full of lightning bugs or Fort Knox gold. The Yellow Jacket was trimmed in the accent colors of red, black, and green. These accent colors tried everything possible to subdue the ever brilliant and glowing yellow. Yet the yellow… Yes, that yellow-set the jacket off and made it an absolute rarity.

Pee Wee and I (AKA Doc, with the real name Clyde) were the best cousins and friends. My dad, Richard Sr. (AKA Red) and Garrett's dad, James Sr. (AKA Jimmy) were brothers, close friends and coworkers at Coppertone, Plough Inc. They were two of ten boys and two girls born to Frederick and Estella Sweeting Hall of Sweeting Town. We were all "best family friends".

Pee Wee and I did as much as two boys could cram into a Saturday. When I visited Pee Wee's home in Perrine, we usually climbed trees two stories high, threw China berries at passing cars, hung out with our Mexican friends and learned a little Spanglish. We also did our part in contributing to cavities with all the cookies and candy we ate. However, this day was not for hanging out with friends or climbing tall trees. Instead, this day was set aside for capturing a Yellow Jacket.

Chapter 4

Did You Hear That? Did You Hear That?!

On this cool Saturday morning, my father and I arrived at Uncle Jimmy's house just as the sun wiped the sleep from its eyes and peeked slowly over the horizon. Garrett and his family had lived in a wooden shack for a long time. Recently, Uncle Jimmy and several of his brothers had built his family a concrete block home. This block structure was built high enough off the ground to withstand the ferocious hurricanes and their potential floods.

The dew-covered grass sparkled appreciating the last moments before the sun's heat and atmospheric humidity became unbearable. For now, a cool, fresh breeze accompanied us as we slipped out of adult eyesight.

Normally, we'd have small change to buy cookies and candy bars at Thompson's Grocery Store or Bell's Short Stop. Not today, for we were traveling light and as quiet as cat burglars. Words were left behind as we walked quickly towards the yawning, stretching, warm, and smiling sun. After several blocks of brisk walking, Pee Wee suddenly stopped dead in his tracks.

"Doc, Doc!" He shouted, "Did you hear that, did you hear that?!"

"Hear what?" I said while looking dumbfounded.

"That crow! Listen, Doc, just listen!"

All was still—so still that I couldn't hear a crow– but my pounding heart beat in my ears! I could hear the wind softly blowing through the tall pine trees and the rustle and bustle of the town waking up, but I couldn't hear a crow.

Suddenly, I saw the wind shift in the top of the tall pine trees. This shift was accompanied by silence and complete calmness. The ever-faint sound I heard was not what I learned in my first grade reading book. You see according to that book; all roosters made a crowing sound of cock a doodle doo. The sound I heard was quite different from a cock a doodle doo…

It seemed natural that I recognized it as a rooster and not a dog, cat, or some other animal. This was a sound of declaration and challenge. It was equivalent to the angry roar of a lion or the snarling of an angry dog. It came as a test to see if we were listening and if we were ready to learn another lesson. Not a cock a doodle doo, but a deep throat, low and irritating, "Er-er-er—errrrr!" It came as an act of defiance and arrogance to let us know who was in charge. Behind this cockiness and fearlessness was an animal who had previously matched wits, courage, and strength with Pee Wee and his other friend Woody. This rooster had gotten away from them more than once and it showed in his deep throat crow of disrespect to the new invader of his space.

This was the Yellow Jacket (AKA Jacket), and he was irritated with his persistent conquistador, Pee Wee. You see, before my arrival this morning, Pee Wee had crowed to call out Yellow Jacket. The animal returned Pee Wee's crow which made the rooster aware that a new quest was about to begin.

Pee Wee was as excited as a toddler at his own birthday party. He threw his head back and answered Yellow Jacket with a hearty er-er–errrrrr! He then leaped with joy when Yellow Jacket returned his crow—errrrrrrrrrrrr! Pee Wee's eyes were sparkling with excitement that ignited and heightened my desire to see and capture this rooster. A vivid picture of Yellow Jacket had been painted in my mind and I was looking forward to the chase.

"That's him, that's him, Doc, that's him!"

But how do you know that it is him? I asked myself.

As if to answer the disbelief that registered on my face, Pee Wee blurted out, "I know that crow anywhere!"

Unlike Richmond Heights, where I lived, West Perrine was a small town where the rural lifestyle was prevalent. There you would hear roosters crowing, hens cackling, pigs oinking, witness cock fights, learn of an OK corral shootout at the local bar, see man made mountains and rain filled holes that offered hours of endless fun.

Here children would play hide and seek, adults would ruin cars in the craters called potholes, and unpainted shacks unfit to inhabit would have large gardens to make ends meet. Also in Perrine, there was serenity, peace, strong families, hard working adults, a little boy's heaven and of course– Yellow Jacket. Adults expected us to entertain ourselves. If we said, we were bored, then we were given something constructive to do, like read a book

Chapter 5

The Secret Weapon

I had never chased a rooster before, but it was clear that I had been recruited because I assured Pee Wee that I was faster than Woody. I was as arrogant as Yellow Jacket and felt that today he would be good as caught. The pursuit was going to be like the first time I rode a bike or the first day of school; no big deal. I was in for a rude awakening because Yellow Jacket had a secret weapon that gave him a proven plan of escape.

Pee Wee knew Yellow Jacket because he had chased him countless times and lost. In the past, when Pee Wee lost, he did not have his secret weapon to catch

Yellow Jacket–me–the Doctor. As a young kid I was a speedster who successfully competed in the AAU (Amateur Athletic Union) Track Association. Yet, I was in for a big surprise.

Other roosters like Big Pete, who had a huge red and blond colored plumage, had been captured. Yellow Jacket was not a one-eyed fowl like Pete or a slow strutting chicken like Big John. Yellow Jacket was special because there was not one rooster in Perrine like him. So, Pee Wee became obsessed with his capture. More than once he had come within inches of reaching out to grab the slippery fowl and each time Jacket would escape right out of his grip.

Yellow Jacket was uninterested in being caught and having his freedom taken away. He was irritated that Pee Wee hadn't gotten the message because he had no problem outsmarting Pee Wee and Woody on several occasions. Like Yellow Jacket, I felt that I was just as smart as him. In fact, I was too smart not to catch him. Heck, I made straight As in school, with an occasional B. I had book smarts, but Jacket had life skills and he used these skills to remain free.

Jacket's secret weapon was not revealed to me until later and this omission led to my cockiness. This chicken was fast– real fast and he was smart– real smart, and he had a stealthy weapon that he knew how and when to use. Pee Wee already knew this and although he didn't tell me, I was about to find it out real soon.

Er er errrrrrrrr! Er er errrrrrrrr!

Jacket, like Pee Wee and me, had egos the size of the city of Perrine. Each time Jacket called back to Pee Wee, it was clear to see that Jacket's voice was moving further and further away from us. Once again, a lesson learned. Jacket knew Pee Wee was tracking him, so he moved to safety. Each crow revealed that he was putting more and more distance between us and our egos. Despite Jacket's strategy, his ego was his biggest flaw and he continued to answer Pee Wee as if to say, "Come and get me."

I was hyped, anxious and as excited as a puppy when its owner returns from a long day at work.

Let's go get him," I shouted to Pee Wee!

"Noooooooo Doc, you stay here."

"Stay here? What do you mean stay here? I can catch Jacket by myself."

I was confident that Pee Wee and Jacket were acquaintances. They had played this game of chess and chase before, and Jacket was signaling Pee Wee to "let the games begin." As these two combatants made their moves, it was interesting that no other rooster dare crow—not one! The other roosters seemed to know that avoiding Pee Wee meant maintaining their freedom for another day. Only Jacket seemed cocky enough and up to the challenge, while the other roosters sat back and waited for the sparks to fly.

Yellow Jacket had led us to the edge of a heavily wooded area with a blanket of pine straw, pine stumps, sharp rocks, and snakes on the forest's floor. Jacket's past strategy was to set the stage on a terrain that was beneficial to him. Thus, giving himself a huge advantage before the chase even began.

A thousand battles are fought and won in the minds of great warriors even before the combatants are arrayed on the battlefield and the warfare begins.

In the past, Woody and Pee Wee chased Jacket simultaneously. Because they got tired at the same time, the rooster was able to escape. Past victories boosted Jacket's confidence, so he was ready to use the same strategy today.

"Stay here Doc, I'm going into the woods to find him and run him out to you." Pee Wee's new surprise strategy was not to have both of us tired out at the same time. He would chase Jacket to me and pass the pursuit off like a relay baton.

Once inside the woods, Pee Wee called out to Jacket again. Soon after Pee Wee entered the woods the sounds that the contest was now underway filled the air. Jacket's loud squawking, flying pine needles, pinecones, and dust from the palmetto underbrush could be seen and heard all over Perrine. This sound seemed to cause all to pause as if this was a Cassius Clay (AKA Muhammad Ali) vs. Sonny Liston rematch.

I could hear Pee Wee and Yellow Jacket as they ran past every palmetto bush. Pee Wee was hot on Jacket's trail and Jacket was heading right to me. Jacket didn't seem so sure of himself anymore. His cockiness really sank when he exited the wooded area, and I was awaiting his arrival. There was a sense of urgency in his eyes when he exited onto the black top country road. Pee Wee had it "on the bottom" and was matching Jacket in speed and moves.

When Pee Wee entered the woods, Jacket crowed for him to come and get him. Well now Jacket was wild eyed and seemed amazed at this change in Pee Wee's strategy.

When Jacket saw me, he put it into overdrive and sprung his secret weapon.

My fresh legs had me so close that I could smell what he had eaten for breakfast. As I reached out to grab him and do what Pee Wee and Woody could not, Jacket suddenly went from running to flying, from squawking to smiling, and flapped his wings right out of my hands.

So, this is the Jacket... what a stunning creature, more beautiful than words can describe. Men have fallen in love with beautiful women, fast cars, speed boats, fishing, sports, and power. Pee Wee fell in love with a chicken! Not the goose that laid the golden egg, not Mighty Mouse, or Under Dog– but a chicken.

Chapter 6

Born Free

Jacket was a kaleidoscope of colors so brilliant that it appeared God had painted him and set every feather in place. This animal's spirit was so free that it felt criminal to be pursuing him. Yes, the colors were made in heaven and delivered to earth by Yellow Jacket himself. Momentarily, I was a mere spectator at such a glorious creature.

The capture of Jacket was Pee Wee's dream! Although this was Pee Wee's delight, I felt compelled through his persuasion and every fiber of my being to assist him in realizing it.

"Get him Doc, get him," were the words that helped me get over Jacket's beauty and his secret weapon [his ability to confidently fly and escape). I went from being outdistanced by Jacket's flying to becoming Bob "Bullet" Hayes.

Hayes was the 1960 100-meter Olympic gold medalist and the only human on the planet to also win a Super Bowl ring. Jacket saw the awe and respect leave my eyes, which was replaced by deadly aggression and laser focus. My determination helped wipe the smirk off Jacket's face. Pee Wee was supposed to be tired, but he was way too hyped! Pee Wee's new strategy of flushing Jacket out of the woods to a fresh pair of legs and lungs then running Jacket until he was tired had not entirely kicked in.

More than once I reached out to get this varmint and he would simply kick it into overdrive and fly away. We chased Jacket into a nearby yard, he ran and hid beneath bushes momentarily he then began to fly beneath the hedges. We chased him then he ran faster and flew each time out of our outstretched hands. He flew until it was clear to him that his flying was becoming an advantage to us. We did not have to run in a crouching stance anymore because the hedges were preventing him from a vertical flight.

Like a good prize fighter, Pee Wee and I had cut the yard off and narrowed down the area of the chase to a much smaller portion. I was able to catch Jacket's wing, but the fight was not over because he was able to spur me, peck me and once again slip my grip and escape.

"Doc, chase him to the fence and let's pen him in," Pee Wee shouted!

Chasing him to the fence meant that Jacket would continue to run in and out of the hedges. It also meant that the fence and hedges would become our ally, as Jacket would not be able to use his secret weapon anymore.

We were on either side of Jacket now with the fence on the third side. He was cornered and had nowhere to go. We were all panting hard and exhausted, and we all were about to have a life changing experience. Jacket was squawking so loud that the angels in heaven must have paused to see what all the fuss was about.

An old lazy dog in the yard had sat and watched this craziness, but he seemed too afraid to even bark. The homeowners never saved Jacket by telling us to leave their yard either. Jacket had no allies and he had met his match today. He was caught by a strategy that he had not planned on. He was also caught by a strategy we had not planned. Our chase was strictly improvisation as we thought that Jacket would be caught as soon as he exited the woods. Instead, we used the available resources at our disposal. The yard, hedges, fence, and lack of interference from the dog and the homeowner all worked together to catch Jacket. None of it was planned. We simply improvised like John Coltrane and Miles Davis.

When I looked into his eyes, they made me sad that after an exhausting and strategic chase we caught him just to cage him and display his beauty for only a few and not for many. His victory crow would not be heard in Perrine today or ever again because this was his last stand.

Author's Historical Perspective

The Hall boys caught a rare creature whose beauty lied in the eyes of the beholders. They cut off the future aspirations of this beautiful creation by capturing him then caging him. They separated him from his freedom, familiar surroundings, his kind, his offspring, and his personal confidence with total disregard for his right to exist unbothered by us.

All these factors were controlled by a wooden crate and their selfish desires. The real moral of the story has everything to do with catching a rooster and nothing at all.

There is a striking parallel to the era, which I grew up in during the 1950s and 1960s and this actual event. I was told by the elders that there had been signs posted in Miami during the 1950s which stated, "Nigger read and run, if you can't read, run anyhow."

Blacks were called coloreds and negroes. The natives of the Caribbean Islands were not allowed on Miami Beach, in Coral Gables or certain other locations without work permits. I remember having segregated accommodations called Colored beaches, Colored water fountains, Colored restrooms, separate but unequal Colored schools and other such woefully inadequate resources. Most of us "kept our places" as if we were caged like chickens. In our midst there were some Blacks who wouldn't hear of "staying in their place." Some would be as defiant as Yellow Jacket refusing to relinquish their inalienable rights without a fight. My maternal granddaddy, Tanny Gaiter would boldly take his family to the "White" beach in Ft. Lauderdale. He had fought for the freedom of Europeans 1,000s of miles from Miami.

When he returned home, his freedom still was denied and deferred. Being the only licensed Black plumber and a war veteran didn't amount to a hill of beans. Grandpa Hall wasn't sitting on the back of the bus and staged a sit in each time he rode the bus; long before Mrs. Rosa Parks decided to stage a sit in. Of course, as a biracial Jamaican it was difficult to tell his ethnicity. For him "having a drop of Negro blood" did not disqualify him from pursuing his happiness.

Some Blacks refused to be denied full access to the pursuit of happiness and were labeled as troublemakers and criminals. "WE THE PEOPLE" were harassed, investigated, arrested on trumped up charges and/or assassinated by those who were sworn to protect ALL American's inalienable rights.

We do not seem to be considered a full partner in the fellowship of America the beautiful.

We the people are continuously fighting for full access to something that belongs to us. It is given to others without any special conditions or impediments. It is our inalienable rights, but it is withheld, obstructed and or denied to us simply because of skin color. This denial of full access to the pursuit of our happiness makes the premise, purpose, pursuit, and product of our constitutional rights fraudulent. At times, even the amended constitution remains blocked.

A dream deferred is, indeed, a dream denied.

What happens to a dream deferred? Does it dry up like a raisin in the sun? Or fester like a sore - then run…Or does it explode? ~Langston Hughes

Riots are the language of the unheard and looting, burning, personal injury and murder are its explosive consequences!

Freedom always seems free to some but not to others. Like a festering dream dried up the dream is deferred in the Land of the Free and Home of the Brave.

For the most part, racism existed in the public and private arenas of the antebellum south, but it was very much alive in the north. I spent my first six-and-a-half years living on a street with all Black residents. This street was bordered by White neighborhoods on three points and a public park on the fourth border.

The Black children played at the same park as Whites and used most accommodations without incident. Some of the things that were happening in Mississippi and Alabama in the 1950s and 1960s, just would not have been good drama in Miami. Many of the Blacks which I knew just wanted equal access, equal accommodations, and a quality unobstructed life.

Errrrrrrrrrrrrrr! Errrrrrrrrrrrr! We needed freedom to ring, but all we heard were crows.

Many didn't care as much about desegregation or integration as they cared about equitable access to public resources. All of them seem to know that one would not come without the other. In fact, I had waited patiently to become a George Washington Carver High Hornet. Others had waited patiently to become Mays High Rams. This patience did not pay off because these Black segregated high schools were phased out and Black students were shipped off to mostly white schools.

Caged Choices

In 1968, I was being bussed to a school that I did not want to attend. Freedom caged and liberty denied was nothing to crow about, especially when our inalienable rights were not fully granted or recognized [just ink on paper].

What does that have to do with catching a chicken? Yellow Jacket was a rooster and not a garment worn by Snoop Dog, Super Fly or your prom date. Unlike Jacket, Jim Crow was not a fowl, but a foul and legal means of caging Black's freedom while denying them full access to the liberties in the United States Constitution. Many White Americans who enjoyed constitutional freedoms every day of their lives were obsessed with denying Blacks that same right. Their obsession with freedoms denied for Blacks was no different than the obsession Pee Wee had for catching and caging Yellow Jacket.

So, the foul Jim Crow laws presented a kaleidoscope of rules that were as brilliantly constructed as Yellow Jacket's coat of colors. Constructed to dishonor a specific demographic of America's people with the blessing of the US Government.

The foul Jim Crow was used to deny access to people of color, especially Blacks.

Many of the red, yellow, and brown "coloreds" of America were able to assimilate and disappear into America's fruited plains and purple mountain majesties. White immigrants who came to America had greater access to the American Dream on their first day of arrival to America than many Blacks who had been here all their lives.

Yellow Jacket did not show any physical scars of his capture. Some Blacks were captured, caged, displayed, enslaved, legislated against, last hired, first fired, executed and auctioned for the greed and love of money. Today's Blacks show no physical scars from the previous generations of our ancestors. However, there remains psychological scars from a system which is still geared to cage freedoms and keep Blacks in a place disconnected from full access to their inalienable rights.

We have been told to forget what happened in our history and move on. In fact research shows that as of 2019, many do not want to hear anything about slavery and its adverse impact. Others have said that to continue to discuss American history will cause our country to take a step back and become even more divided. I believe a man who does not know his history, is destined to relive it repeatedly. https://www.pewresearch.org/fact-tank/2019/06/17/most-americans-say-the-legacy-of-slavery-still-affects-black-people-in-the-u-s-today/

The Jewish Defense League's objective is to track down Nazis that killed Jews during WWII. WWII ended nearly 80 years ago and it also ended 80 years after the Civil War. No one tells Jews to just forget about their history and move on. No one tells the southerner to just forget about his confederacy "heritage". So, the confederates continue flying the confederate flag and celebrating traitors who tried to overthrow the US government to form their own. And Blacks keep paying taxes to maintain confederate memorials and to provide security for KKK marches and confederate holiday celebrations.

God told the Israelites never to forget their history which included bondage in Egypt. He told them to recall their years of bondage through oral tradition and to write how they were delivered from bondage in their hearts and in their homes. They were told to remember their deliverance each day, but we are told to stop causing divisions.

Therefore, to remember is not to stir up hate, to remember is to have a lesson standard that reminds, warns, corrects, and prevents recurrence.

Memorials should make us better as humans, not bitter.

Epiphanies of Childhood Innocence

Nevertheless, like Pee Wee and Doc, some people chase their dreams between the hedges of life. Always planning, but never able to see their dream fly and get off the ground. Some people's lives are improvised without any designed plans. Impulsive, reacting to what is presented and using it to build their response.

Year after year people chase their dreams and just when they reach out for it, the dream flies away. Just when their dreams are in reach, the Klan kills Blacks and burns Rosewood to the ground. Just as their pursuit of happiness is being realized, the US government and domestic terrorists burn "Black Wall Street" to the ground and kill many of its citizens. Just as their dreams were in reach, an assassin's bullet smashes into the dreams of President John F. Kennedy, Attorney General Robert Kennedy, Social Activist Rev. Dr. Martin Luther King Jr., International Activist Malcolm X, and Activist Medgar Evers.

Just when the dream is attainable, Miami- Dade police officers beat businessman Arthur McDuffie to death for a traffic violation. Just when the dream is in reach, James Byrd is chained and dragged behind a truck flinging his body parts over the roadside of Jasper, Texas. Just when the dream is in reach New York's finest policemen ram a wooden handle up the rectum of an African dreamer plunging his pursuit of happiness into the fiery pit of the American nightmare. Just when the Pee Wees and Docs of America reach out to realize their dreams, they are mowed down with 41 bullets in the foyer of an apartment building located in the state of New York. The dream is mowed down in a hail of bullets in a wrong house raid in Miami-Dade, Detroit and anywhere, USA. The location and faces change, the skin and senseless murders/injustices don't.

Dream deferred; festered and running like a sore.

How can you dismiss the past when the past keeps touching the present and the future?

That's what Yellow Jacket was crowing about. That all creatures should be as free as he is and covered by the golden coat of constitutional law whose brilliant contents should apply to all and not the chosen few. All Americans should all be able to crow about how a source as powerful as our sun has positively impacted our efforts to become better humans.

Freedom should be free to all and no one should be fighting for something that is as natural as drinking a glass of water or breathing fresh air.

Er er errrrrrr! Er er errrrrrr! Er er errrrrrr! Oh the sound of freedom.

GLOSSARY

1. **Adaptations** - changing individual or group behavior in order to survive the environment.

2. **Antebellum** - existing before a war; especially existing before the American Civil War.

3. **Anxiety** - uneasiness caused by fear or danger.

4. **Big House** - was the plantation owners' home usually where domestic slaves lived.

5. **Bob "Bullet" Hayes** - was an Olympic gold medalist sprinter who then became an American football wide receiver in the National Football League for the Dallas Cowboys (for 11 seasons). Bob Hayes is the only athlete to win both an Olympic gold medal and a Super Bowl ring. He was from Jacksonville, FL.

6. **Bosom** - intimate or confidential , warm closeness; someone cherished

7. **Conflicted** - opposing or clashing ideas.

8. **DNA** – Deoxyribonucleic Acid - The molecular basis of heredity.

9. **GI.** -Government Issued, a member or former member of the armed forces

10. **Good Humor Man** - a male who sold ice cream products changing the mood to cheerful.

11. **Highlighted** - to emphasize or make prominent.

12. **Irish Twins** - two infants born within twelve months of each other.

13. **Mandated** - an order, decree or command.

14. **Manicuring** - to trim or cut meticulously.

15. **Maternal** - relatives who are related through the mother.

16. **Mindset** - a fixed attitude or state of mind.

17. **Morgan Silver Dollar** - Minted from 1878 to 1904. The first silver dollar minted after the Coinage Act.

18. **On the bottom** - a figure of speech that means to go really fast.

19. **Perseverance** - determined to persist in pursuing something.

20. **Persistence** - to continue, steadily or firmly in spite of obstacles, opposition or criticism.

21. **Psychology** - the science of human and animal behavior.

22.   **Retiring** - withdrawing from contact with others.

23.   **Subtly** - In a way small and difficult to notice but important.

24.   **Suburb** - a district lying outside a city.

25.   **Tin Tub** - A metal tub used to wash clothes and small children.

26.   **Transition** - a period of change from one position to another.

27.   **Trek** - to travel or migrate.

28.   **Vicinity** - the area which is nearby a place.

About the Author

Clyde Hall is a Florida native by way of Dade County (Miami), but his adopted county is Alachua (Gainesville). He is a professionally certified educator, mentor, and now a published author. Mr. Hall's debut literary work, *The Secret Weapon* was written and rewritten over at least two decades.

The Secret Weapon is a children's book based on an event taken right from the pages of Clyde's life. His life courses from living in abject poverty of the 1950s and 60s to being independently wealthy in the character traits that matter more than silver and gold. A wealth of traits that make children strong; confident, stable, goal oriented, respectful, and grateful while living life with a purpose.

Clyde's love for writing is also highlighted and extended in well over 100 poems with themes consisting of social justice, social injustice and spiritual empowerment. His future publications are reflective of his 25 years in sworn and non sworn law enforcement. His poetry and short essays are next on his bucket list to be published by this recent retiree.